To MaryJo,

Best wishes for a happy birthday. I hear you appreciate some of these pieces. So here is the whole lot. I am glad to share them with you.

June 28, 1983

Ray W. Rosevear
M.W.W.

The
Midnight
Wanderer

The Midnight Wanderer

poetry by

Ray W. Rosevear

A Lyceum Book

Carlton Press, Inc.　　　　　　　　　　New York, N.Y.

©1981 by Ray W. Rosevear
ALL RIGHTS REVERVED
Manufactured in the United States of America
ISBN 0-8062-1327-2

FOREWORD

The material for this book is from the accumulation of occasional pieces over a period of some forty years. No attempt has been made to present them in chronological order.

Many poems came from personal experiences or evolved from a word, phrase, or sentence from friends or acquaintances, but all represent the author's ideas. One, "To a Wastepaper Basket," uses some phrasing and rhymes from the author's sister, now deceased. "America Singing" was written as narration for presentation at a P.T.A. meeting by a high school choir and a speech class in 1943.

The six-line pieces were titled to indicate that no specific relationship exists between any one and any other. They were used as an exercise for each to fit a set pattern of form, line, and rhyme.

The book's title is partially explained by the poem "Midnight Wanderer." Ideas often began on those nighttime walks. Some were completely developed. Most were completed with writing and rewriting by night work at desk, table, or bedside stand.

This selection has been submitted for publication at the urging of some friends and relatives who had the impression that at least some of them were good enough to print. The author, with his ego thus boosted, was inclined to agree.

CONTENTS

Scandal	11
Moonlight on the Snow	12
Midnight Wanderer	13
A Wish from a Rumble Seat	14
There Was No Sound	15
If the Night Be Dark	16
I Still Shall Fight	17
I Bumped	18
Goodnights	19
Memories and Dreams	20
The New Dress	21
Viewpoint	22
Kitten	23
Hills of Cuba	24
Orinoco—A Fantasy	25
In Memory of Joe	26
To the Trailing Arbutus	28
Alone	29
Watching God	30
Awake at Night	32
Music Came to Life	34
Wind Through the Pines at Liahona	36
A Cheer for Spring	37
To a Wastepaper Basket	38
Sounds of Spring	40
Bees and Orchards	41
Night Flight (A Gaggle of Geese)	42
America Singing	46
Speech	56
Disaster	57
Help	57
Lost	57
Blame	58

Hills	58
Sometime	58
Saving	59
Mojave	59
Desires	59
Hope	60
Love	60
Thoughts	60
Incentive	61
Clouds	61
Pud	61
Bluejay	62
Tumbleweed	62
Initials	62
Plans	63
Verses	63

The Midnight Wanderer

Scandal

The new moon walked, last night,
Beside a silver star
And told her things we've no notion of
Away from her so far;
But, oh, the trees were closer;
They heard each whispered word,
And then they told the bushes
The things we never heard.
The bushes kept the secret,
And I made up a song;
But the oak trees whispered gossip
About it all night long.

Moonlight on the Snow

A silvery sheen of light subdues the earth;
A bed of white is spread out on the ground;
The moon is full, and earth lies deep beneath the snow;
The peaceful calm and weight of frost is all around.

A shaft of light is lying on the snow,
A brilliant stretch across the crust of white.
It shows a path where trembling shades are in the depths,
And sparkling jewels of ice are on each little height.

The distance blurs and seems to be up close;
Some leafless trees are holding up the sky;
The lonely house out on the hilltop's but a blot
Against the distant place where earth and heaven tie.

A symphony of silence reigns tonight,
The music of all nature still and cold;
The moon is busy for a moment with a cloud,
And shadows come. It seems that shadows are so bold.

Midnight Wanderer

A midnight wanderer am I,
Seeing things that others see by day.
I've strolled along the country lanes
Watching willows holding roads at bay.

I see the city streets alone,
Knowing well each house with fence or tree,
A kind of loneliness I feel,
One that crowds out cares and sets me free.

For years I've made these nightly jaunts—
Youth, through middle-age, to golden years.
No other exercise seems right;
Walking more befits us sonneteers.

On land, at sea, I've walked at night,
Wrapping up thoughts of the day's end;
I tie up problems in a knot;
Toss them off for someone else to tend.

Perhaps folks think I love the night.
Time to think my thoughts and be alone
Has given me richness that
Reaches out to everything I own.

The setting, rising, suns are friends;
Night birds talk to me. They seldom sing.
The moon at quarter, full, or new,
Constellations change from fall to spring.

So, rain or snow, through heat or cold,
Vision restricted by the dark,
I'm dressed to go out wandering now.
Mind is clear, I would remark.

A Wish from a Rumble Seat

I wish I had a piece of the sky,
A piece of blue and white
That stretches out beyond all reach
Of thought and sight.
And then, to give a definite sense
Of balance, each bright day
I'd like to have a little patch
Of white and gray.

But when I see the skies at the close
Of day, I'd like to hold
The title to the strip that's silver,
Red, and gold.
And, oh, for one more piece—and it's high
Above my head tonight,
With stars and moon and mist
In silver light.

I wish—and there's the sky to share.
I merely need to reach and claim
The little piece or two I'd like
And build my castle in the air.
But wait—before I take them out,
I think I'll look behind the sky
And see what's there.

There Was No Sound

There was no sound that I could hear
Except the beating of the rain,
And each pulsation gave me pain
As there I sat with no one near
To share my sorrow or to cheer
My thoughts. To speak aloud was vain.
There was no sound that I could hear
Except the beating of the rain.

Then softly to an inner ear
Your voice spoke words that still remain:
"Faithful until we meet again."
Though memory made love more dear,
There was no sound that I could hear
Except the beating of the rain.

If the Night Be Dark

The blackness of so strange a night as this
Has come and blotted out all thoughts of past
And hollowed out a void so dark and vast
There's naught remains of memory's doubtful bliss.
A night has settled o'er my life's abyss;
No single ray of light now dares forecast
An end. With all light gone, I can't contrast
The present dark with light I thought I'd miss.

What matter if the night be dark, so long
As light of past and future disappear?
Oblivion's eternal joys belong
To him in solitary darkness. Here
Are life and death both made immensely strong
By balanced power. Let darkness now appear.

I Still Shall Fight

In the gray dawn of hope alone I stood
Where night had left me wounded, all but dead;
The battleground was somewhere in a wood
Where trackless, pathless doubt and fear had led
Me long, and black despair like flames of Hell
Had tortured mind and soul and broken all
Resistance save that hope alone might well
O'er come and make these blackest hours fall.

I still shall fight—shall fight for consciousness
And an awareness—happiness or pain—
Oh, I must feel, must know, must have access
To depth and height of all I can contain.
To know, I still shall fight and reach my goal
To win, this once, give all but life and soul.

I Bumped

I bumped against the past and barked my shin,
Then stumbled on a dream and nearly fell.
I found that the way out is also in,
And learned I knew much less than I could tell.
I took the long leap forward to escape
And landed back near forty years ago.
Measuring life with an uncertain tape,
I came up short in happiness and woe.
I'm finding there are never short ways back,
And neither is there time to stop and stare.
Most things are never always white or black;
But that pertains to neither here nor there.
    Fair weather comes on either side of storms;
    Lost time is found again in other forms.

Goodnights

I know I need not say to you, "Goodnight,"
And still again goodnight in thought or word;
But were you here just now, I'm sure we might
Find ways to say goodnights that could be heard.
But you have gone to where I cannot come
And view a mansion that cannot be mine.
The past we had was but a partial sum;
There is no future, now, nor bottom line.
Once more I call to mind the things we knew,
The words we spoke, the days and nights we shared,
The many years we might have had, we two,
And all that could have been had we but dared.
    What was is was—and end without an end;
    And goodnights now must ever be pretend.

Memories and Dreams

I know I should forget about you now,
But memories are difficult to shed;
They cling like white oak leaves upon the bough
When leaves of other trees lie brown and dead.
But dreams are like the needles of the spruce;
When one drops off, another takes its place;
And winter seems to say, "Oh, what's the use?
With them I have no chance to win this race!"
With distance, time, and death I live these days.
Eliminating one of them will not
Effect a major change; for still my ways
Of life will be as though I just forgot.
   The memories more frequently will blur,
   But dreams repeatedly will still occur.

The New Dress

You asked me to tell if I liked it;
To be truthful, I told you, "No."
I might better have lied and endured it
Than to see you turn, crying, and go.

To be honest is better, they tell me,
And a lie is never quite right;
But I'd rather see you wearing it
Than to have you out of my sight.

So come back, and I'll tell you, "I like it."
And I'll tell you—not to be kind—
"I'll be looking at you, not the dress, dear."
To be happy, we must sometimes be blind.

Viewpoint

A frozen, hidden lake was to my right,
And to your right, a grove of maple trees,
As heart to heart we stood in dim starlight
With thoughts of past and future things to please.
There in the wondering silence of our minds.
"What do you see?" we asked each other then.
Why did we want to know, as if it binds
Each to some final grand amen.

You said Polaris; but Orion, I;
The fixed star yours, the wandering hunter mine.
That's been our life together. Though we sigh,
We've never both seen quite the same design.
You've wanted all things fixed and permanent;
I've sought a change, whatever that has meant.

Kitten

Little kitten in the rain,
Mewing softly at our feet,
Wanting love; if not that, care,
Milk to drink, and food to eat.

Coming here to us as friend,
Little kitten in the rain,
Lonely, ragged; cold and wet,
You've not sought for friends in vain.

You have found us; we've found you.
As you purr while getting dry,
Little kitten in the rain.
We will visit, she and I.

We must part; so now goodnight,
Wondering if we'll meet again;
Strangers met, but part as friends,
Little kitten in the rain.

Hills of Cuba

What lies in the hills of Cuba?
What lies beyond that shore?
My ship lies still in this harbor.
I want to see much more.

We're here in Cienfuegos
To load our empty ship.
Then when the holds are all loaded,
We'll start the homeward trip.

Like stars in an early evening
Against a dark-blue screen,
White houses show on the hillsides
Backed up by hazy green.

Through shimmering heat of August
Those hills invite me there;
Beyond the landscape of city
There must be clean, fresh air.

I won't get out to the country;
There's someone I must meet
When I'm ashore in the morning
And walk the city street.

This ship's crew's keeping me busy
At this and that and such.
With all of the things I'm doing
I won't be seeing much.

Some day I'll come back to Cuba
To walk among those hills;
I'll learn of the plants and people
And visit the sugar mills.

Orinoco—A Fantasy

Riding on a sliver
Down the Orinoco River,
    I met a man
    Who had a plan
To get my living liver.

Riding in a fliver
By the Orinoco River,
    I had to ride
    To save my hide
From an Indian Indian-giver.

A-tremble and a-quiver
In the Orinoco River
    I had to dive
    To stay alive
As mad maidens made me shiver.

Working with a siever
In the Orinoco River
    I left my place
    To plead my case
To a lying lie-forgiver.

A cargo to deliver
Up the Orinoco River,
    To save my life
    I took the knife
From a skinny, skiving, skiver.

In Memory of Joe

My friends, the Baileys,
Had a dog named Joe.
Joe liked to bark at car wheels
And to bite at people's heels
All the time;
And whenever folks came to visit,
Joe was there to greet them.

He'd bark at them a little while,
Then keep still
Until they thought he'd gone away;
But just as they'd open the door
To go into the house,
He would sneak up behind them
And nip their heels a little.
Joe didn't do it because he was mean
Or anything like that.
He just wanted some fun.
But even dogs become victims
Of plans men devise—
Sometimes.
So I always carried some
Tidbits to keep Joe busy
At something else
When I went into the house.
He'd work for minutes to shell a peanut
Or to chew a gumdrop.
But he didn't mind;
Neither did I.
And he got so he expected something different
Of me.

Joe is gone now,
And people can get to the house
Without the fear of God—or dogs—
Put into them.

But I miss Joe,
Even if I didn't like him much.
Besides that,
In my car, I still have some candy
That belongs to Joe.

To the Trailing Arbutus

No other flower seems brave enough to bloom
In April. Long before the grass is green
Or budding trees dress up for spring, you show
A tender pink and white in contrast to
The rotting, crackling leaves of autumn's last
Discard. Almost before the snows are gone,
Your rough green leaves adorn a sunny slope
Or knoll, and faint pink buds peep out to catch
An ultra-violet ray or two and set
To work to turn them into fragrance and
A color that will match at least the best
That any other season can produce.

Yes, you, arbutus, rough and lowly plant,
But always first. No other dares to show
Herself to dangers of a frosty night
And chilling damp of slowly melting snow.
Your sole companion in a chilly wood,
The hardy wintergreen whose little fruit
Now ripe and pithy from the winter's rest,
Had bloomed last year to give a fruit this spring.

The freshness of an April wind you burst
Your buds to beautify a deadened world.
To scent anew the warming Easter air
Foretelling heaven in a month to come.
You give a hidden world your very all,
Then push along new shoots in readiness
And promises for yet another spring.

Alone

Alone tonight, alone;
No one to talk to,
No one to listen to,
No one to look at,
No one to look with;
No one has been near;
No book to read,
No picture to look at,
Not even a radio for company.

The moon has gone away for a week or two;
The leaves on the trees won't rustle;
Animals, big and little, have hidden themselves;
Even the insects are silent;
The light has gone out and won't be back;
The wind shut the door with a departing sigh.
It's so quiet one could hear a pin drop.
But I haven't any pin.
The clock stopped an hour ago;
My watch hasn't run for a week.
My pen has reformed and won't scratch as I write.
Only I—alone tonight.
Alone.
But I LIKE it!

Watching God

I saw a flash of lightning far away
As storm clouds gathered fast around.
I asked myself then, as the sky grew dark,
If God, the owner of the earth, would stretch
Forth both his hands to pull the clouds apart
To take a look at his choice property
Before he let the rain descend on it.
Of course, there is no answer to my thought;
But still I think that we see God when we
See lightning in the sky.

                                                  A brighter flash!
Then God spoke words with thunder-voice. I'm sure
He told the animals, the plants, the stones,
That they had grown too dusty from the earth.
The drops began to wash the faces of
The trees and scour every blade of grass.
I stood and saw God scrub the earth and sky
To wash them clean of dirt and dust and grime;
He used the soap of force applied so well
By fingers, hands, and arms of gusts of wind.
God washed the world, then hung it in the sun
To dry.

                        When his day's work was all complete
And God began to clean up for the night,
He stood before his mirror on a wall
Of sky and held it so that I could get
A look to see his image in the glass.
You may have seen no more than moon that night
But it reflected God to me.

                                        Somewhere
I'm told, a heaven lies above us in
The sky, and God lives there in glory, light,
And power. That may be so—I half believe
It true. This universe of ours is oh,
So old. The roof needs patching right away.
Look up there where the stars shine bright. They're not
The worlds we often think they are. Those stars:
Holes in the ceiling of the universe
Where light from heaven keeps shining through all night.

I've heard God watches all that happens on
This spinning earth of ours. Creation once
Begun, goes on now all the time; and God
Must oversee the work of man and beast.
It's true, I s'pose; but all the time that God
Is watching me, I'm watching him.

Awake at Night

Awakened at night from a dream-infested sleep, I lie in the intimacy of a solid dark that enfolds one as tightly as the embrace of a lover.

Sleep is gone, having fled my eyelids like a startled fawn that stands for a breathless moment to understand the cause of its fright, then leaps the thicket and bounds into the underbrush to be gone, yet to remain near enough to watch, waiting for a chance, perhaps, to return.

Out of the black and nowhere, thoughts come pouring in like many grains from a variety of storage bins are poured into a huge feed mixer.

But the thought bin, if not bottomless, is so vast and deep that it gives that impression as the grains of ideas rush past, seeming never to fill it.

And the supply is so constant and varied that it at least borders on infinity.

Mental fingers reach out to catch a thought, perhaps of school a new procedure for a history class, and gets hold, in the rush and dark, of an idea for a teachers' party.

Or, reaching after a kernel of God, come up with a doubt from Hell.

A walk in the woods turns out to be a campfire and marshmallows.

A star becomes a calendar, a theater becomes the skies; a boat ride, a swim; a walk, a road in the autumn woods or a snapshot.
Or a Greig concerto changes first into a phonograph record, then a bridge across a winter stream, which becomes an embrace or a perfume.
A recent movie becomes a Nelson Eddy-Jeanette McDonald duet that becomes a conversation on a hidden park bench with the full moon shining through white pine branches.
There are sounds that press as heavily against the ears as the darkness does against the eyes, the faint humming of dark silence.
Crickets go unnoticed, and are themselves a part of the still quietness.
And, because the mind, seeing others, wanting all, yet failing to grasp any, soon has a firm hold on a great nothingness.
Looking at nothing, hearing nothing, attention lags, a drowsiness releases the dark and silence.
The pressure of emptiness is released; out of its nothingness comes a dream again and reality.
Sleep has overcome the wakeful; the thought bin is gone; the startled fawn has returned to its sweet pastures.

Music Came to Life

Until we began—casually at first—to speak of music of records and composers, of symphonies and overtures, of operas and prima donnas, of. . . .

Music was a sound—a pleasant sound—that fitted well into the moods a person had, or helped to produce the desired effect when used appropriately as background for a radio program or for reading a poem.

A symphony was a Sunday afternoon of reading or dozing with the radio turned on, waiting for the intermission talk of some commentator, usually Deems Taylor.

An opera was a Saturday afternoon of reading or wondering what the foreign words meant; of trying, mentally, to picture action on a stage; it was remembrance of fourteen hours of unbroken labor as a stagehand for the opera company in a one-night stand production of *Aida* at the teachers college.

Music was not of the soul, not of the intellect, not of the emotion.

Music was memory of an existence. It was a platform filled with instruments and men, and the name Sousa on the program; it was a high school band marching in the hot sun and dry dust for a Fourth of July; it was pages in a book and lines and dots and words on a sheet; it was "Rock of Ages" and flowers, or "O, Promise Me" and flowers or "The Old Time Religion" without flowers.

But our talks, casual at first, about it, made music come to life.

It may have been so many things from you that touched a hidden chord with me; your enthusiasm for music, your appreciation of the music in everyone, ("No monotones," you once said) your saying, "Good music for every child"; your willingness to spend an hour after school each afternoon helping children learn to play the piano; it may have been. . .

Nay, it was! But it was much more.

It was hearing you play, and watching you play, when I should

have been correcting papers.
It was watching you write music for songs to be sung at a P.T.A. meeting.
It was learning from you that a symphony has four movements—and what a movement is.
It was learning that Schubert's *Unfinished Symphony* was really the way Mr. Schubert meant it to be.
It was learning to pronounce ' Kammenoi-Ostro" correctly.
It was listening to records and talking about them with you.
It was learning the meening of "chords" and "scales" and other music terms like "opus" and "fugue" and "concerto" and listening to music like that.
It was meeting composers as friends rather than as history or as names on a sheet of music or on a phonograph record or from a radio speaker.
It was. . .
These things it was, multiplied by a thousand, that helped me to hear music, to see music, and to feel music, knowing what I heard and felt, knowing until I felt compelled to exclaim silently and within myself at the closing strains of one symphony: "O, music, thou art mine; let me but be thine!"
Music became, from our conversations, a wood thrush's song, the nervous flight of a humming bird, the dripping of rain on a tent roof, the shadow of an oak leaf on the page of a book, the kiss of a loved one in the shade of a pine under the full moon.
It became speeding cars, roaring motors, black smoke and red-hot iron, people getting off buses, laughter at a fireside party, the bark of a dog, pages turning in a library, the smile of a child, the waving of an American flag. . .
It became speeches, pictures, people; light, dark, silence, sound, things; earth, sky, stars; air. . .
Music became, not all things, but in all things, around all things, and through all things.
Music came to me
Because we began—casually at first—to speak of music.

Wind Through the Pines at Liahona

Oaks and poplars rustle,
Birches stand there mute.
Pine trees whisper softly,
Gentle, lyric lute.

Pines are dark and somber,
Black against the sky
Filled with stars and moonlight,
Drawing heaven nigh.

Melodies are never
Always quite the same—
Roar, or whispering murmur,
Music without name.

God is watching o'er us;
Liahona guides;
Love is ever near us,
God where man abides.

A Cheer for Spring

A robin or meadowlark wakes us at morn;
And sure as there's sunshine, a new spring is born.

The world is a-tremble; we feel it all day;
From morning to nightfall, its promise is May.

With song or a whistle, a shout or a roar,
There's soul-filling laughter as winter is o'er.

A wind howls in rapture, and children play ball,
Or marbles, or tag, or just nothing at all.

A thunderstorm shouts at the top of its voice
But young folks and old as one person rejoice.

The antifreeze boils from an old Chevrolet;
A backfiring Ford can be heard up the way.

The roar of a motorcycle's soon heard,
A love call in spring days without any word.

So come shout for joy; let spring's praises be sung;
Call out the cheers, boys, if you burst every lung.

The long, frozen winter is on the way out,
For spring is upon us. Let's give her a shout.

To a Wastepaper Basket

You, dear old basket, you're only a bucket or can
Now all battered and scratched and so beat out of shape;
But perhaps by some kindly benevolent man
You've acquired some paint where you once had a scrape.

But though you're all broken and banged in a hump,
You're the dearest, old sweetest, old thing that I own;
I can find down in you about any old dump
That I tossed into you with a smile or a groan.

There's a rind or a husk of some food that I ate,
And a box, or it might be a shoe over-worn;
And some ads that appeared, or a note from a date,
And the scraps of a story conceived but unborn.

There is sand from a shoe which I wore on a hike,
Or a cloth I once used to wipe off the mud;
You've some rusty bent nails, an old railroad spike—
I recall when I dropped it, there was a deep thud.

Could there be, now, a hundred or more worthless things?
If there are, I shan't bother to list them in turn.
You already contain all the mailman now brings,
All except a dear letter that I must yet burn.

There are other things, too, I'm not ready to share,
Not just yet anyway; but someday you'll get all
Of the treasures I've stored in a safe place somewhere;
And to you, old basket, will come the first call.

I have already told you much more than I could
To a very best friend, of my dreams, schemes, or plan.
Oh, I'm sure you accepted and still understand,
For I've stuffed you full daily for such a long span.

You will keep all my gripes, all my moods and my joys;
I can give you much more, and there's more you will get.
So just sit quietly while keeping your poise,
And hold on to your contents should you get upset.

So am I a collector, as you seem to be.
Some folks toss me their regrets and over-supply;
And I'm asked to be blind to whatever I see,
And to reveal to no other each laugh and each sigh.

On occasion I'm battered or tipped or upset;
But I keep to myself all that I've received.
You and I can't be brothers—at least we're not yet;
We will keep what we're given until we're relieved.

Sounds of Spring

Drip and splash, drip and splash;
Ice melts from the river banks.
From a northern window sash
Snow melts off—and gets our thanks.

Chirp and cheep, and whistle, woo;
Insects, birds, and froglets sing,
Coming each at its own cue,
Taking credit for the spring.

Cats out howling at all hours;
Hoot-owls call from on the barn,
Keep their peace, but breaking ours,
Hoping mates believe the yarn.

Little sounds that strain the ear,
Hushed and hallowed part of all;
Lone leaves drop as if in fear,
Rustling those that dropped last fall.

Soft, slow bubbles rise and burst;
Sodden soil makes room to store
Soft clay drops where floods were worst;
Waters splash and wait for more.

Crunch of stubble mix with those
Made by walking through fresh grass.
Hush of spring where e'er we go.
We must listen, hear—and pass.

Bees and Orchards

If you've the time and inclination
And a necessary thing
   (Such as money)
Won't you walk through apple orchards
Where the bees will hum and sing
   Making honey?

So as you stroll through trees and grasses
Slap mosquitoes, flies and fleas,
   (If they're there)
Let the humming bees alone;
Run for shelter if those bees
   Tangle your hair.

Yes, smell the blossoms, see the flowers;
Beauty's free for all who'll see;
   (But some are blind)
Feast your soul in apple orchards;
Cares of winter soon will flee
   Away behind.

Spring trees and bees are some expressions
Of the careful plans of nature,
   (She's not unkind)
Which give us joy in things of beauty.
So keep caution in your pleasure
   Ever in mind.

Night Flight
A Gaggle of Geese

Now! Follow me!
I'll lead!

Hey! Look up there!
A lake!

Look at that moon!
It's round!

Don't go ahead
Of me!

Don't go so fast!
You're mad!

I can't keep up!
Too bad!

Why did we start
So soon?

He's going east,
Not south!

Time to change leaders now!

I think that I
Should lead.

I want to stop
And eat!

You want to stop
And rest!

Oh, did I tell
You that?

How many miles
Today?

Miles are for folks,
Not birds!

You silly goose!
I know!

When do we eat?
I'm starved!

How many eggs
You laid?

I'll bet they all
Din't hatch.

How did you know?
I peeked!

Next time I'll fly
Alone.

You could get lost
That way!

See! There's another Vee!

I'll bet we beat
Them there!

Where is the there?
I'd ask.

Your first trip south?
That's right!

Why must we fly
A Vee?

We always have.
That's why!

That's a good joke
You told!

Even a goose
Can laugh!

I have heard that
Before!

Think you're smart,
Don't you?

Smarter than most,
I'd say!

Hunters below!
Bang! Bang!

Hah! Missed us all,
That time!

Nobody's safe
These days.

Why don't they shoot
Themselves?

Sometimes they do,
I'm told!

Sun's coming up!
Watch out!

Cornfield below!
Let's land!

What a long flight
That was!

Shut up and fill
Your crop.

America Singing

A Program for Choral Reading and Choir

"I hear America singing;
The varied carols I hear."

We are Americans, everyone;
We are the sons of Americans, all.
We sing the songs Americans sang—
Sang as they fought, as they worked, as they played.

Who sang the songs Americans sang?
Who sang the songs Americans sing today?

Did the soldier sing?
Did the schoolboy sing?
Did the farmer sing?
And the laborer?
Did the Negro sing?
And the Indian?
Did the mother and father sing?
And the cowboy?
And the miner?
The sailor?
Clerk?
Photographer?
The. . .
Did they!
Did they SING!

"Listen, my children, and you shall hear."
From the midnight ride of Paul Revere
To the day of Pearl Harbor and after;
Through war and famine, good times and bad,
Through bloodshed and peace conference,
Dust storm and flood,
Sunshine and laughter.

Americans sang!
Americans sang her sorrow and joys;
America sang—her girls and her boys,
Her men and her women
Sang as they fought, as they worked, as they played.

"Listen, my children, and you shall hear."
With fife and drum,
In 'seventy-six
We won our independence while singing.

"We hold these truths to be self-evident
That all men are created equal..."

With fife and drum we sang and marched;
We sang and worked, the whole caboodle;
We sang and fought—to *Yankee Doodle.*

(Choir sings *Yankee Doodle*)

With freedom won and at peace again
The soldier dropped the gun and sword,
Went back to his plow, his farm, and his cow.
He cut the trees to build his home,
And he cleared the land, and he cut the grain.

But war again, to keep our right
To sail the seas.
So farmer and sailor and soldier's son
Once more marched forth to man a gun.

And as they marched and sailed,
They fought and sang.

(Choir sings *You're In the Army Now*)

A hymn was born, in blood and tears,
That has stirred a nation through the years
Our national anthem, the song of the land.
We sing it today. Will everyone stand?

(Choir sings *The Star-spangled Banner*)

But we sang as we worked;
We sang as we played;

We sang in the sun,
We sang in the shade;
We sang on the mountains,
We sang on the plains;
We sang on the highways,
We sang in the lanes.

Folk tunes, work tunes,
Slave tunes, and ballads.

We sang from our lives,
We sang from our souls;
We sang in the tropics,
We sang at the poles.

A man of the people,
Foster by name,
Grew up with the nation.
He listened, and wrote
The songs we were singing.

What did he write?
Was it songs *we* sing?

He wrote *Old Black Joe,*
And he wrote *Uncle Ned;*
Songs of the blacks, at work, at play.

And he wrote of home,
Songs of love and of dreams.
We sing them, and sing them,
And sing them today.

Let's hear his songs,
The old songs,
That we all know so well.
How's this: *Camp Town Races?*

(Choir sings *Camp Town Races*)

Or you may have heard this:

(Choir sings *Oh! Susanna*)

And certainly this:"

(Choir sings *Beautiful Dreamer*)

We fought to get old Texas,
Then made it one huge state.
"Remember the Alamo!" had been the war cry,
And the "Lone Star" still is great.

(Choir sings *The Yellow Rose of Texas*)

The slaves were freed.
All were Americans, now.
Remember, we quoted:
"...All men are created equal."

In heartbreak and bloodshed,
The black was freed.
But the nation, at last,
Stood strong and united.

But soldiers had marched,
And many had died;
They sang, as they fought,
The songs of the side.

The Blue and the Gray are gone now forever;
The nation now stands as one.
The songs they sang are dear to us,
And we sing them now together.
The *Battle Hymn*, or *Dixie*,
Both North and South together;
For over a land united
One banner is unfurled.

And, "Government of the people,
By the people, and for the people..."
Has *not* perished from the earth.

(Choir sings *The Battle Hymn of the Republic*
and *Dixie*)

The black was free,
Free to work, free to play,
Free to preach, free to sing.

From the jungles of Africa,
The cotton fields of Virginia,
The log cabins of Louisiana,
And the church of the unlearned parson,
Came the black man's God.

And they sang to their God of their work;
They sang to keep back the tears;
They sang to forget—and to remember;
They sang and they prayed, and they preached
"De glorious songs of the Lamb."

(Choir sings *Swing Low, Sweet Chariot*)

But America grew up,
And growing, stretched herself.
Her strength was equal to her task,
And singing helped make it so.

The workmen sang in shanties,
In forest, mine, and plain;
Paul Bunyan and his blue ox,
John Henry, Casey Jones.

While on the lone prairie,
A cowhand watched the herd;
He sang of home and heaven,
Or fought and killed and cursed.
From Texas to Wyoming,
From Montana to Nevada,
The cowboy was at home.

(Choir sings *Home On the Range*)

Chug, chug, chug; chug, chug, chug;
Chug, chug, chug; chug, chug, chug;
Clang, crash! T o o o o o o o ot!

New York, Philadelphia, Chicago,
Kansas City, Denver,
And all points west!

America worked, America fought.
America loved and danced and sang.

From the Bowery in Manhattan,
To an Iowa city square
And the band played on.

(Choir sings *The Band Played On*)

We danced to that.
And now, recall
Those horse and buggy days.

What days? When?
Why...

(Choir sings *When You Wore a Tulip*)

The auto came,
The flying machine;
The age of speed was here.
The trusts were busted,
The women voted,
There was nothing, now, to fear.

But
But what?
Listen to *that!*
Listen!
Thump, thump, thump, *thump, thump, thump!*
THUMP, THUMP, THUMP; *THUMP, THUMP!*
WAR!

(Choir sings *Over There*)

And when Johnny came marching home again,
HURRAH!

What then?
Money—but no liquor;
Radio—but static;
Music—and jazz;
Land boom—and paupers;
Stock market—then CRASH!

Depression.
Dark, dreary days;
Walking from office to office,
From factory to factory,
From farm to farm,
From city to city.

Hitch-hikers, technocrats, dust storms, Dr. Townsend...
But always depression— and no work.
Always Depression.
Depression.

Then the New Deal,
And every card marked with the alphabet:
NRA, PWA, NYA, AAA, TVA;
And the whole ABCs.

And sit-down strikes!
But work!
Real work—with wages.

And "Heil Hitler!"
And millions marching, marching marching;
Millions carrying rifles on their shoulders
Because a few insisted on carrying chips on theirs.
Millions marching,
Pausing only long enough to
Give a stiff salute to a trick moustache
And shout, "Heil Hitler!"

But not here!
Here in America we were singing,
Singing and working again.
Swing and symphony;
Blues and opera;
But singing—**America** singing.

But wait!
Why?

Is that **War** again?
Yes, but not here.
"It can't happen here!"
But it **did**!

(Choir sings *Remember Pearl Harbor*)

And we were in!
Working and singing;
Working and fighting;
Working and marching again.

America singing?

Americans will always sing!

So long as there is free air about them,
Or the hope of free air,
Americans will sing.

Sing as they fight, as they work, as they play;
Sing as they love, as they rest, as they pray.

(Choir sings *America*, last stanza)

Speech

A dog that howls
A cat that yowls.
   A parrot that will screech:
With beasts and fowls
We've lots of vowels
   But very little speech.

Disaster

An icy road,
A wind that blowed
　My car into a ditch:
I once was throwed
By a horse I rode.
　One's worse. I don't know which.

Help

Huge drifts of snow,
Cars that can go
　When equipped with chains:
I think so slow,
I need a tow
　Or traction in my brains.

Lost

Noah's Ark,
A fragile bark
　To sail an endless sea:
My soul's lone spark
Must face the dark
　Of long eternity.

Blame

A Model T,
An old elm tree
   That brought it to a halt:
It's plain to see
What's stopping me,
   Is surely not my fault.

Hills

Hills in a row,
Patches of snow
   That reach to hide the ground:
My virtues, though
They stretch and grow
   Scarce hide my faults, I've found.

Sometime

Five times ten,
Or half-past when—
   Whatever time or place:
Someday again
We'll meet and then
   We'll visit face to face.

Saving

A stack of hay
In June or May
   That gives next winter's feed:
I save my pay
And hope someday
   To have the things I need.

Mojave

Forever sand,
Dry barren land,
   With wind and hot and cold:
The view is grand;
On the other hand,
   Few people here die old.

Desires

Money to lend,
Money to spend,
   Money to give away:
Desires tend
To have no end.
   Not so my weekly pay.

Hope

Oh, golly-gee,
How good to be
A friend of one like you:
I now can see
Some hope for me
If what you said is true.

Love

Like sun through rain
Like ease from pain,
  Like a pillar of light:
Gloom is all vain;
Love can sustain
  Us, and life will be bright.

Thoughts

At each sunrise
At sunset skies,
  And under stars at night:
To summarize,
It's no surprise
  My thoughts of you are bright.

Incentive

A moon that's full,
That makes a pull
   Upon the seas and hearts:
When life gets dull,
And there's a lull,
   I need a pull that starts.

Clouds

Clouds like mares' tails,
Or vapor trails,
   Or speckled gray and white:
A project fails,
Effort prevails,
   As clouds are often bright.

Pud

Oh, our dog Pud,
Who walks in mud
   And gets his belly wet:
He's not pure-blood,
Can't be a stud;
   We'll keep him for a pet.

Bluejay

Flash of blue haze,
Eyes of steel gaze,
   A raucous fighting call:
I like blue jays'
Free-wheeling ways.
   I'm not like that at all.

Tumbleweed

A tumbleweed
That sees no need
   To stop and take a rest:
It spreads its seed
With all due speed
   The way that it knows best.

Initials

A memory spot
That means a lot,
   Initials on a tree:
Though mine they're not,
They make a blot
   Where no blot ought to be.

Plans

Plans gone awry,
An alibi
   That keeps me in the clear:
Though truth I try,
Sometimes a lie
   Is all folks want to hear.

Verses

Verses for self,
No thought of pelf,
   Nor gain in any way:
Put on a shelf
Like precious Delft,
   They're what I have to say.